P9-DGC-545

GREAT MYSTERIES

SEA MYSTERIES

The sea has always played an important part in
stories about mysterious events. There are tales
about ships vanishing or being found without any
of their crew aboard; about sailors seeing, or even
being attacked by, monsters of all shapes and sizes;
and about the "Bermuda Triangle," where planes as
well as ships disappear. Some of these cannot be
true, but others . . . As you read this book, try
to decide which events have happened and
which are just sailors' stories.

GREAT MYSTERIES

SEA MYSTERIES

Ben Wilson

Illustrated by Tony Gibbons
and Martin Kingstone

The Bookwright Press
New York · 1989

Great Mysteries

Ancient Mysteries
Monster Mysteries
Sea Mysteries
UFOs

Cover Illustration: A sea serpent attacks some whalers who have tried to capture it.
Frontispiece: One of the most famous sea mysteries concerns the *Marie Celeste*, which was discovered drifting in the Atlantic Ocean on December 3, 1872 without any of her crew. The ship that found her sent some sailors aboard, who could find no clues to explain why the *Marie Celeste* had been abandoned.

First published in the
United States in 1989 by
The Bookwright Press
387 Park Avenue South
New York, NY 10016

First published in 1988 by
Wayland (Publishers) Limited
61 Western Road, Hove
East Sussex BN3 1JD, England

Library of Congress Cataloging-in-Publication Data

Wilson, Ben.
    Sea mysteries / Ben Wilson.
        p.   cm. — (Great mysteries series)
    Bibliography: p.
    Includes index.
    Summary: Presents mysteries of the world's oceans, including lost treasures, pirates, sea monsters, shipwrecks, wartime sinkings, and explorations.
    ISBN 0-531-18249-5
    1. Curiosities and wonders — Juvenile literature. 2. Sea stories — Juvenile literature. [1. Curiosities and wonders.   2. Sea stories.]   I. Title   II. Series.
G557.W55 1988   88-6896
001.9'4—dc19   CIP
                                                                AC

Phototypeset by Oliver Dawkins Ltd, Burgess Hill, West Sussex
Printed in Italy by G. Canale & C.S.p.A, Turin

Contents

The secrets of the sea

A coelacanth *from the Indian Ocean. This species of fish is over 60 million years old and was, until recently, thought to be extinct.*

The sea is the last great mystery that faces us here on earth. For even as we take our first hesitant footsteps into outer space, much of the underwater world, which makes up over 60 percent of the earth's surface, remains unexplored and unknown to us. Humankind has mapped out the world's ocean surfaces, sailed the seven seas and built submarines to travel beneath the waves. But our knowledge of the geography of the ocean bed and of the countless varieties of creatures that inhabit this world below the waves is still relatively limited.

The sea keeps its secrets well. Only recently it was discovered that the *coelacanth*, a bluefish dating from 60 million years ago and thought to be extinct, still thrives in the Indian Ocean. Do other sea creatures dating back to prehistoric times still roam the ocean depths? Could some of the reported sightings of gigantic sea monsters actually be true?

Perhaps the sea also hides clues to our own past. Legends tell of a beautiful, fertile island called Atlantis, which seems to have flourished some time between 10,000 and 1500 BC. The island was rich in minerals and vegetation and its people were extremely advanced in the sciences and the arts. However, it appears that Atlantis was completely destroyed in the space of 24 hours by a volcanic explosion and sunk beneath a tidal wave.

A diver exploring a wrecked ship off the Philippines, in the Pacific Ocean.

Did Atlantis really exist? Do its ruins lie somewhere on the ocean bed? There have been many claims for and against the existence of the city of Atlantis. Some people have claimed that the legend of Atlantis really refers to the ancient Minoan civilization, which was based around the island of Crete in the Mediterranean Sea. Others still insist that the ruins of this once-great civilization lie beneath the waters of the Atlantic Ocean. Edgar Cayce, a so-called visionary, claimed that Atlantis was destroyed in the year 10,000 BC by a huge explosion and that its true location was near a small island in the Bahamas called Bimini. Some years later, a number of stone structures were found off the coast of Bimini, but experts are divided about whether they

6

are natural rock formations or the remains of walls of an ancient civilization.

The sea jealously guards a wealth of fascinating secrets. There are strange tales of the puzzling disappearance of ships and people in certain sea areas, of ghosts and ghost ships coming back to haunt or curse the living, of seemingly impossible sea voyages made long ago, and of treasures lost in the mists of time. These are the mysteries we will now set out to explore.

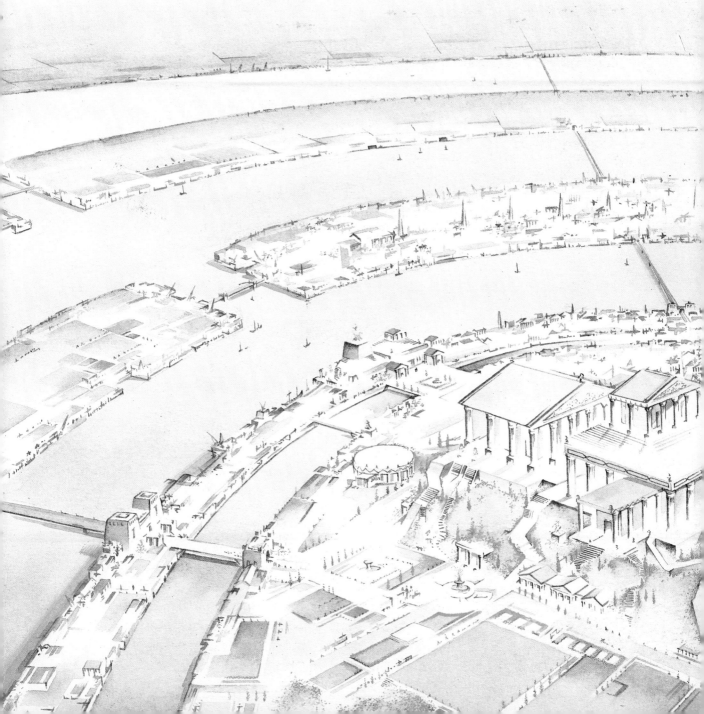

The legendary city of Atlantis probably looked like this before it was destroyed by a large wave or an explosion.

Vanished without trace!

It is March 4, 1918. World War I still rages on land and at sea. In the waters of the western North Atlantic, a 19,000-ton supply vessel, called the U.S.S *Cyclops*, leaves Barbados and sets sail for the American port of Norfolk, Virginia.

In command of the *Cyclops* is German-born Captain Worley, a man well known for his strange behavior. On leaving Barbados, he inexplicably orders the ship to turn suddenly to the south, away from the planned route.

Then, without warning, all contact with the *Cyclops* is lost. An air and sea search finds no trace of the *Cyclops*, nor is there any sign of wreckage. It seems that no German submarines or mines were in the area at the time of the ship's disappearance.

What happened to the *Cyclops*? Was it struck by a freak wave or blown up by bombs planted by German spies? Was it betrayed by its odd captain? An official U.S. Navy investigation rejects these explanations, calling the incident "one of the most baffling mysteries in the history of the Navy."

One fascinating theory remains: that the *Cyclops* became yet another victim of the mysterious region through which it traveled . . . the so-called Bermuda Triangle.

The ships' graveyard

The area in which the U.S.S *Cyclops* disappeared has been called "the ships' graveyard." Its actual name is the Sargasso Sea, and it lies in the western region of the North Atlantic. Its most striking feature is the masses of seaweed that float on its surface. Sailors' legends tell of how ships were held forever in this web of weeds or were sucked beneath the surface in its deathly grip. Whatever the truth of these tales, there have been a series of baffling losses of ships in this region since records were started in 1800.

At the beginning of the nineteenth century, no less than three ships were mysteriously lost in this region in the space of 25 years. On August 20, 1800, the U.S.S *Pickering* and her crew of 90 disappeared while heading for Guadeloupe, a group of islands in the Caribbean. Fourteen years later, the

Crewmen from the Ellen Austen *set out to investigate a schooner that was found abandoned near the Azores in 1881.*

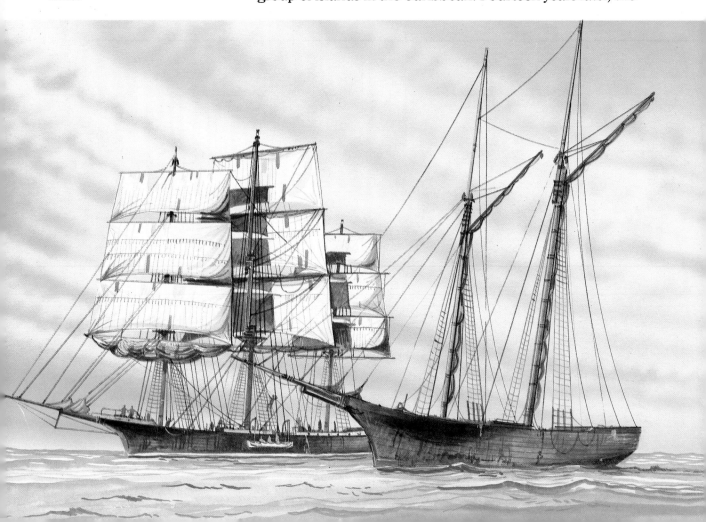

The "Philadelphia Experiment"

Could an experiment, said to have been carried out in 1943, provide a clue to the secret of the Bermuda Triangle? It was designed to test the effects of a strong magnetic field on a manned ship. The results were amazing. At first, a hazy green light surrounded the vessel. Then, both ship and crew began to disappear! Soon, all trace of them had gone! Only after the magnetic field was switched off did they become visible again! It is even said that, for some months afterward, members of the crew were prone to vanish and then reappear! Are magnetic forces the key to the Triangle's mystery?

U.S.S *Wasp* vanished without trace with 140 men aboard. Then, in 1824, the U.S.S *Wildcat* and her crew of 14 disappeared shortly after setting sail from Cuba.

Ships have also been found adrift, abandoned by their crew for no apparent reason. In 1881, the *Ellen Austen* was passing west of the Azores when her crew came across an

In 1945, five planes, like these, mysteriously vanished over what was later to be called the "Bermuda Triangle."

abandoned schooner. Three men were placed aboard the schooner, but soon afterward a storm blew up and she became separated from the *Ellen Austen*. When she was sighted two days later, the three crewmen had also disappeared! A second crew of three went aboard the schooner. Once again, a sudden storm separated the two ships. This time, however, they were never to meet again. The schooner and her crew had vanished, leaving behind a mystery that remains unsolved to this day.

It was in 1945, after five planes vanished while on a routine training flight, that this strange region began to attract worldwide interest. Shortly before contact with the planes was lost, the pilots reported that their instruments were "going crazy," that they had lost their bearings and that they were "entering white water." Because their flight path had followed a triangular route, whose apex was in direct line with the island of Bermuda, the region became known as the "Bermuda Triangle."

Even with the aid of modern technology, no one can explain the strange power of the Bermuda Triangle to swallow up ships and aircraft. But what is it like to experience this frightening and unknown force? Captain Don Henry was in charge of a tug that was towing an empty barge to Fort Lauderdale, Florida, in 1966. The sea was calm and weather conditions were good. Without warning, the tug's compass began to spin wildly. Then, in Henry's words, "the horizon disappeared — the water, sky and horizon all blended together. We couldn't see where we were." The barge was enveloped in a milky-colored cloud, while the sea around it became choppy and disturbed. At that moment, the tug's electrical power failed. It was slowly being pulled back into the cloud. Henry pushed the tug's throttle full ahead and, after a long struggle, managed to pull the barge clear. Later, he said that it had felt like "being pulled in two directions at the same time."

What theories have been offered to explain the mystery of the Bermuda Triangle? It has been suggested that violent underwater currents may suck ships to their doom in seconds or cause huge tidal waves to overwhelm them. Some have even claimed it is UFOs, which hijack the ships and kidnap their crews in order to examine them. Do the remains of an ancient civilization that had advanced powers lie within the Triangle? Does it still send out pulses of

Other mysterious disappearances

1880 HMS *Atlanta* and her crew of 290 cadets disappear without trace.
1902 A German ship, the *Freya*, is discovered adrift with no crew on board. They are never found.
1932 The *John and Mary* is found abandoned in perfect weather conditions only 80 km (50mi) from Bermuda.
1963 A huge freighter, the *Marine Sulphur Queen*, disappears.
1973 The *Anita*, a 20,000-ton freighter, is lost along with her crew of 32.

In 1966, Captain Don Henry's tug, Good News, *was almost sucked into a mysterious milky-colored cloud while sailing through the Bermuda Triangle.*

energy that cause havoc to the surrounding seas and skies? Or is the true explanation that the area is subject to strange magnetic forces that can cause planes and boats to vanish and be whisked to another time and place?

Perhaps these ideas are merely the product of people's imaginations, and there is a simple, more logical explanation for these disappearances, which has been overlooked or ignored.

The Flying Dutchman — fact or fiction?

In the early seventeenth century, Captain Hendrik van der Decken sets sail from Amsterdam aboard the *Flying Dutchman*. He is bound for the East Indies. A greedy and foolish man, he is determined to make his fortune on this trip.

All goes well until the ship begins to round the dangerous waters of the Cape of Good Hope. For days fierce storms batter the ship. In spite of the pleas of the passengers and the crew to seek sheltered waters, Captain van der Decken heartlessly pursues his course. He drinks and smokes, pausing only to fill the air with curses.

Suddenly, a strange form appears on deck. It announces that it is the Devil and challenges van der Decken to oppose God's will by sailing into the teeth of the storm. The Dutch captain agrees . . . and brings down God's curse on his head:

> "You are condemned to sail on until the Day of Judgement, without rest and without ever making land."

From that day onward, the *Flying Dutchman* is doomed to roam the seas, bringing ill fortune and disaster on any vessel that might cross her path. The tale of the ghost ship seems to be the stuff of legend. But there are numerous accounts of people who claim to have seen her . . . and suffered as a result!

Ghosts and ghost ships

The sea has been a place of danger and death for many sailors. As a result, a number of superstitions and legends have arisen about those lost at sea and the ships they sailed in. Most of these, of course, are the work of many a sailor's vivid imagination, told and retold with ever more fantastic details added. But there remains a handful of genuinely puzzling, ghostly sea mysteries that still send a tingle of fear down the spine.

Mystery surrounds the tale of the *Ourang Medan*, a Dutch freighter that was bound for Jakarta, Indonesia, in February 1948. On a day of calm seas and clear blue skies, she sent out the following SOS call, which was picked up by over a dozen ships:

> "Captain and all officers dead. Entire crew dead or dying. Now I am also near death."

A grim sight awaited the rescue team that reached the stricken vessel three hours later. The deck was littered with

Was it a horrific monster that terrified the crew of the Ourang Medan *to death in 1948? We will never know.*

corpses, while on the bridge lay the dead bodies of the officers and the captain. Each man appeared to have died in the same way, eyes fixed in horror and arms raised to the sky. Even the ship's dog lay with its fangs bared and its paws arched in the air, as if trying to ward off an invisible enemy. The rescue team's doctor could find no trace of poisoning, or disease or of any fumes that might have caused the deaths. What was the cause? The question has never been answered satisfactorily.

Why should a photograph of two men swimming in the Pacific be one of the most remarkable ever taken? Because the two men, James Courtenay and Michael Meehan, had been killed four days before the photograph was taken! They had been overcome by poisonous fumes while working in the engine room of the oil tanker, *Waterton*. On December 3, 1929, the day after they had been buried at sea, an astonished deckhand spotted the two men swimming just 15 meters (50 ft) from the tanker. Over the course of the next three days, the men were to appear frequently, smiling and waving at their astonished crew mates. On the tanker's next voyage, a member of the crew managed to take eight photographs of Courtenay and Meehan. Unfortunately, only one of the photos gave a clear picture. But, it was enough. Friends and relatives of the two men had no doubt that the two swimmers were Courtenay and Meehan!

Perhaps the most best-known sea mystery is that of the *Marie Celeste*, the "ghost ship" found adrift off the Azores on December 3, 1872. There was no sign of life on board, either above or below decks. There were no clues to explain why the crew had disappeared. Indeed everything appeared to be quite normal. In the crew's quarters, clothing lay folded neatly on bunks, and washing hung on lines. In the galley,

One of the photographs taken of Courtenay and Meehan, swimming next to the tanker Waterton, *after they had been killed by poisonous fumes in the ship's engine room.*

The ghost ship of the Goodwins

The *Lady Lovibond* ran aground on the Goodwin Sands, off southeast England, on February 13, 1748. At the time a wedding celebration was being held on board. Fifty years later to the day, a three-masted schooner identical to the *Lady Lovibond* was seen heading toward the Goodwins. Voices and laughing could be heard, followed by screams of terror as she ran aground. On both February 13, 1848 and 1898, the same ghostly sight was seen, and the same sounds of joy followed by horror. In 1948, many people watched for her, but nothing was seen. Will she return in 1998?

breakfast had been prepared and some of it had been served. In the captain's cabin, breakfast had been left. Next to it, the captain's log showed entries up to November 25 and gave no hint that anything was wrong.

Why was the *Marie Celeste* abandoned? It seems unlikely that bad weather was the cause. There was little sign of damage on deck and the ship had taken on only a normal amount of water. Was there a mutiny? There was no sign of a struggle and, in any case, why would the mutineers have left the ship too?

Instead of answers, there remains one final question. How did the *Marie Celeste* remain on her intended course for eight days and some 800 km (500 mi) with no one at the wheel to steer her? Stories grew up that the ship was cursed. Although she was recovered and put to sea again, she had an unhappy history. She was sold 17 times in 11 years before being run aground deliberately off the coast of Haiti in 1884, taking her terrible secret to a watery grave.

What made the captain of the Marie Celeste *abandon his ship half-way through his breakfast?*

The ghost of the UB65

The Second Officer of the German submarine UB65 was killed when one of her own torpedoes accidently exploded in her hold. For months after the accident, the Second Officer was seen by members of the crew in different parts of the submarine. One crewman was driven mad by the ghost's presence and threw himself overboard to his doom. Even a pastor could not rid the submarine of her unwanted visitor. Finally, on July 10, 1918, just as the UB65 was about to be attacked by an American submarine, the German vessel was ripped apart by a terrible explosion from within. Could the ghost of the UB65 have taken its terrible and final revenge?

Crossing the Atlantic . . . in a boat made of reeds!

As the coast of Central America comes into view, Thor Heyerdahl, the Norwegian adventurer and scientist, has good reason to feel happy. Many people have ridiculed his claim that the ancient Egyptians could have made the perilous journey across the Atlantic over 2,500 years ago in boats made of papyrus reeds. But now he has proved it was possible by completing the voyage from Morocco to Central America in a reed boat.

Heyerdahl used detailed drawings made by the artists of the ancient Egyptian Pharaohs. These showed every stage of the making of the reed boats, from the way the reeds were cut, bundled and lashed together, to the design of the steering gear and the layout of the rigging.

Heyerdahl's first attempt to make the crossing was in 1969, in *Ra I*. The journey was full of difficulties because the raft became waterlogged in rough weather. Finally, the eight-man crew was forced to abandon the 17-meter (56-ft) craft when it was struck by a freak wave only a short distance from its goal.

However, just two years later, *Ra II* successfully completed the voyage with relatively little trouble. Heyerdahl proved that ancient civilizations could have made contact with one another, thanks to the slender papyrus reed and the skill of the Egyptians.

Who "found" America?

A painting of Christopher Columbus, the famous explorer. He lived from 1451 to 1506. The native Americans (or "Indians") were, of course, the first people to discover America. But was Columbus the first European to sail there?

Most of us are familiar with the story of Christopher Columbus's historic voyage from Spain to the shores of America in 1492. He bravely defied dire warnings that, by setting a continuous course to the west across the Atlantic, he and his ships would fall off the edge of the world or be consumed by savage sea monsters. Instead of meeting such a fate, he actually opened up the route to the New World, although he thought at first that it was the East Indies. Columbus is therefore looked upon as the person who "discovered" the vast continents of North and South America. But is this claim true? There is evidence that other people visited this "new world" long before Columbus.

Some archaeologists believe that the earliest sea voyages to these continents were made by the Chinese and Japanese, crossing the Pacific as long ago as 3000 BC. They have uncovered Japanese-style pottery of that period in the coastal regions of Ecuador. Several sculptures, seemingly of Buddhist idols, have also been unearthed in South America and have been dated at around 2000 BC.

A sixteenth-century painting showing Columbus arriving in North America. Was he the first European or had other people beaten him to it?

One person who may have reached North America before Columbus was Saint Brendan. He and 14 other monks crossed the Atlantic Ocean in AD 540 in a boat like this one.

Similarly, could ancient Mediterranean peoples, such as the skilled sea-going Phoenicians and Carthaginians, have successfully made the perilous journey across the Atlantic? The philosophers Plato and Aristotle both wrote of a marvelous and mysterious overseas land first visited by the Phoenicians in 1000 BC and kept a closely guarded secret for trade purposes. Other legends describe thrilling voyages across a vast ocean beyond the Pillars of Hercules (Gibraltar) to lands of great riches. One of these, dating from 500 BC, describes a voyage through slow-moving waters which sound similar to those of the Sargasso Sea:

> "No breeze drives the ships, so dead is the wind of this sluggish sea . . . there is much seaweed among the waves; it holds back the ships."

Perhaps the strangest claim concerns Saint Brendan, an Irish monk who is said to have set sail for the "land promised to the saints" in a 12-meter (40-ft) wooden boat covered with

23

The Vikings, it is thought, crossed the treacherous Atlantic Ocean from Europe to North America in ships like these.

oxhide in the year AD 540. Details of the voyage are recorded in a tenth-century Latin manuscript. This tells of how Brendan and his 14 colleagues set sail from Ireland on a northerly course and passed "floating towers of crystal," sailed through thick fogs, came across strange sea creatures and landed on two small islands before reaching their promised land. Was this land North America?

Although many of the details contained in the story seem incredible, it is thought that Brendan did actually make such a voyage. Some experts believe that his route took him to Greenland, the Newfoundland Banks and the small island of Labrador. He then skirted the coast of North America, stopped off at an island in the Bahamas and ended up in the area we now know as Florida.

We may never know for sure whether Brendan's epic travels really took him across the Atlantic, but it does now seem certain that another legendary sea journey was based on fact. The Norse sagas, written in the mid-fourteenth century, tell of the dramatic adventures of the heroic Viking leader, Leif Ericson. Around the year AD 1000 he led a convoy of Norse ships on a spectacular journey that took in Iceland, Greenland and, finally, North America. The description of the geography, climate and wildlife of the new land contained in the Norse sagas match those of Newfoundland. Recently a stone village dating back to Viking times has been discovered in northern Newfoundland. Could this village be the physical proof that Leif Ericson led the Vikings to America?

The question of who really did first sail the seas to "discover" America may never be answered with certainty. Columbus may have "sailed the ocean blue in 1492" to set foot in the New World, but perhaps he was only following in the wake of a string of skillful navigators and valiant explorers who had made the journey before him.

A statue of Leif Ericson. According to the Norse sagas, he led some Viking ships across the Atlantic in AD 1000. They arrived in North America after visiting Iceland, Greenland and Newfoundland.

A sea monster's deathly grip

The year is 1942. Lieutenant Cox's thirst grows worse under the fierce sun. For three days, he and 11 other British sailors have been adrift in a flimsy life raft in the remote and dangerous waters of the South Atlantic.

With horror, Cox sees a threatening dark shape in the water alongside the raft. It is at least 8 meters (26 ft) in length and has a broad head.

"Am I imagining things?" Cox wonders as he makes out two large eyes staring at him from beneath the waves.

Then, slowly and deliberately, a number of enormous tentacles emerge from the water. They reach out and coil around a man at the rear of the raft. Cox and the other men struggle to pry him free from the vise-like grip of the tentacles. But all their efforts are in vain. The poor victim is lifted from the raft like a baby from a cradle. He disappears, wrapped in the monster's arms.

Cox and his men, wounded in the life and death struggle, prepare for another attack. The creature clearly has the power to crush the life raft and devour all on board. But, incredibly, it does not return. Cox, along with only two other naval officers who survive, will live to tell this frightening tale.

What kind of creature was it that attacked the life raft on that fateful day in 1942?

Monsters of the deep

From the earliest times there have been stories and legends of strange and frightening sea monsters capable of bringing death and destruction to those who dared to venture into certain remote and unmapped areas of the oceans. Norse legend named one of these creatures the "Kraken," a type of squid or octopus so huge that it could overturn fishing boats, whaling vessels and even larger ships. This frightening creature had thick, long tentacles with huge sucker pads and rows of claws to grip its prey, while its "mouth" was a beak capable of cutting through wire and of piercing the side of a ship.

Could it have been a Kraken that attacked a fishing boat off Newfoundland in 1873? The two fishermen on board had prodded what appeared to be a large mass of seaweed heading for their boat and were horrified when it reared up

A painting of a huge, octopus-like Kraken attacking a merchant ship in the late eighteenth century.

in the water and seized their vessel in two huge tentacles. It looked like a large squid or octopus. Repeated blows with an axe eventually forced the wounded monster to release its deadly hold on the boat, leaving behind a piece of tentacle 6 meters (20 ft) long. Experts calculated that it belonged to a creature 20 meters (66 ft) in length.

John Starkey reports a chilling encounter with a Kraken-like creature that came alongside his naval patrol ship in the Indian Ocean one evening in 1942. He recalls "two cold green eyes" staring up from the water, tentacles half a meter (20 in) thick and describes the creature as being longer than the ship — at least 50 meters (165 ft) in length! Fortunately, the monster made no attack.

Other ships have not been so lucky. In 1872, the crew of the steamer *Strathowen* claimed they saw "a giant squid" topple a 150-ton schooner, the *Pearl*, and drag it beneath the waves. In the 1930s, a 15,000-ton tanker called the *Brunswick* claimed to have survived three attacks by Kraken-like monsters.

Another monster of the deep is the giant sea serpent. One is said to have been spotted by the crew of HMS Daedalus *while they were rounding the Cape of Good Hope in 1848.*

There have been many reported sightings of another legendary monster of the deep, the sea serpent. The most famous of these occurred in 1848, when sailors aboard HMS *Daedalus*, a 19-ton frigate, spotted a strange creature while rounding the Cape of Good Hope. Captain Peter McQuhae later confirmed that it was a sea serpent, 20 meters (66 ft) in length, which swam alongside the *Daedalus* for over 20 minutes. The body was dark brown. Its head was raised about three feet out of the water, revealing jaws large enough to hold a full-grown man and lined with fierce jagged teeth.

In 1852, the whaling ships the *Monongahela* and the *Rebecca Sims* were scouring the Pacific when a whale was sighted. Three longboats were lowered from the *Monongahela* in pursuit of the creature, which proved to be huge — some 45 meters (150 ft) in length. Stuck with harpoons, the creature's wild thrashing smashed two longboats, but after a fierce struggle it was hauled alongside the ship. It was too long to take on board, so only the remarkable head with its cruel teeth was cut off and preserved in a pickling vat. However, the *Monongahela* never reached home. Both ship and crew disappeared. Wreckage was found off the coast of Alaska several weeks later. There was no explanation. Was the ship attacked and

Opposite *This map shows where sea monsters, of all shapes and sizes, have supposedly been sighted over the years.*

A sea serpent, with a head like a turtle's, was said to have attacked a life raft in 1962 and carried off four of its occupants.

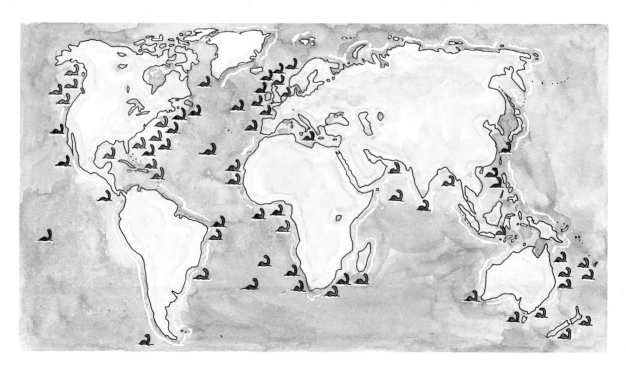

destroyed by yet another monster?

In 1962, a life raft carrying five men was attacked by a sea serpent. Its head and neck resembled that of a turtle and stretched over 4 meters (13 ft) out of the water. Hissing horribly, it gave off a foul-smelling odor of rotting fish. After capsizing the raft, the monster carried off four of the men, leaving one survivor to recount the terrifying tale.

Below *A photograph of "Morgawr," a monster reportedly seen off the coast of Cornwall, southwestern Britain, in 1976. It was about 8 meters (26 ft) long.*

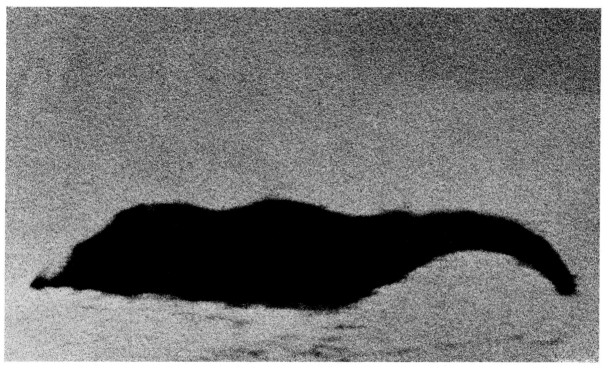

The *Architeuthis*

In 1857, the Kraken was given a Latin name by scientists, *Architeuthis*. The largest specimen ever measured was washed up on the beach in St. Augustine, Florida, in 1896. Its tentacles measured about 9 meters (30 ft) and its original length was estimated to have been 20 meters (66 ft). Many sailors claim to have seen giant *Architeuthis* doing battle with sperm whales. One captured sperm whale had sucker scars measuring 36 centimeters (14 in) on its body, suggesting that its foe measured around 150 meters (495 ft) – half the height of the Eiffel Tower in Paris!

Above *A sea serpent that, it is said, was seen frequently off the coast of Massachusetts in the 1800s.*

Right *A nineteenth-century picture making fun of people who said they had seen monsters at sea.*

Some sea monsters choose to haunt waters closer to land. One such creature is supposed to roam the Strait of Georgia, between Vancouver Island and British Columbia, off the west coast of Canada. It was first sighted by native North Americans long before white settlers arrived, and is known as Cadborosaurus or "Caddy." In this century it has been seen by over 100 people and has been described as being a sea serpent 15 meters (50 ft) long, with huge, wide jaws.

In 1965, a Belgian zoologist, Dr. Bernard Heuvelmans, began the most detailed study of sea serpents to date. He examined 587 sightings, dating from 1639 to 1964, and concluded that 358 were genuine. From these, he divided the sea serpents into nine types. Could the oceans really be roamed by so many species of sea monster? If so, how many more are yet to be discovered?

Monsters sighted around the world

1882 Llandudno, North Wales: "a large, dark, undulating creature as big as a large steamer."

1893 Cape Town, South Africa: "a giant eel, 25 meters (82 ft) long, with jaws 2 meters (6.5 ft) wide."

1964 Great Barrier Reef, Australia: "a gigantic beast, 20 meters (66 ft) long, with jaws 1 meter (3.3 ft) wide."

1966 North Atlantic: "a writhing, twisting monster, from 10 to 12 meters (33 – 40 ft) long."

1976 Cornwall, England: a monster, nicknamed "Morgawr" (sea giant), measuring about 8 meters (26 ft), is photographed.

The quest for le Vasseur's treasure

The year is 1730. As the notorious French pirate, Olivier le Vasseur, climbs the gallows and a noose is placed around his neck, he lays down a challenge, "Find my treasure who can!" With these words he throws a chart to the spectators. The chart, and other papers of le Vasseur found later, contain strange diagrams and messages written in code. Who could unlock le Vasseur's secret?

For over 200 years the mystery remained unsolved. Then, in 1949, Reginald Cruise-Wilkins is shown some papers and a number of rocks on a beach at Bel Ombre in the Seychelles. Similar weird markings have been made on each of them. After studying the markings, Cruise-Wilkins feels sure they are the clues left by le Vasseur. He believes he can interpret them.

Following the directions in the papers, Cruise-Wilkins begins to dig at Bel Ombre. At several sites he finds buried statues and carvings. A pattern begins to emerge: each site stands for one of the 12 labors of the mythical Greek hero Hercules.

After 20 years of searching, Cruise-Wilkins reaches the site of the twelfth labor. It is a cave, marked by a carving of Cerberus, the three-headed dog who guarded the Underworld. Cruise-Wilkins is convinced that le Vasseur's treasure lies beneath it. However, he died before he could dig it up.

Lost treasures

How many treasures still lie in sunken wrecks at the bottom of the ocean waiting to be discovered? A great many it seems. Modern bounty hunters now use the very latest high-technology equipment to seek out underwater treasure troves. For these scavengers of the seabed, there are rich pickings to be won.

But time and tide still defy even the efforts of these experts. The *Lutine* was wrecked off the coast of the Netherlands in 1799. Because of the dangerous storms and treacherous tides that occur in this region, her rich cargo of gold, silver and banknotes to the value of several million dollars is largely untouched. Over the years, the wreck has become covered with silt and sand, so its precise location is no longer known.

Similarly, a British vessel, the *Grosvenor*, foundered while rounding Cape Horn in 1873. Her cargo of gold and jewels would be worth over a million dollars today. Yet all efforts to locate the wreck have failed and it seems doubtful that anyone will uncover her lost treasures.

The Lutine *foundering on rocks off the coast of the Netherlands in 1799. Her cargo of about four million dollars has never been recovered.*

Between the sixteenth and eighteenth centuries, the high seas were a place of great danger for ships carrying valuable cargoes. Pirates roamed the most frequently used trade routes, seeking out galleons bearing valuable cargoes. The most successful pirates would hide their ill-gotten gains in secret locations, often on remote islands. Popular legends quickly arose concerning these burial sites. One such legend is about Isla del Coco, which lies in the Pacific, 560 km (336 mi) from the coast of Costa Rica.

It seems that treasure was brought to the island on at least three occasions. In the seventeenth century, an English pirate named Edward Davies landed seven boatloads of booty there. A few years later, eleven million dollars worth of various treasures was hidden on the island by another pirate, Bonito Benito. Then, in 1821, an English captain named Thomson seized a cargo of treasures that he was supposed to be transporting to Spain on board his ship, the *Mary Dear*. Once again, the dense forests of Isla del Coco were chosen as the hiding place.

The pirate Edward Davies landing on Isla del Coco, in the Pacific Ocean, where he is meant to have buried seven boatloads of treasure.

It seems that these treasures were never recovered by the pirates. As a result, a number of bounty hunters launched expeditions to try to find them. The most successful of these was a carpenter named John Keating, who recovered a huge fortune in gold in 1844. Auguste Gissler spent 17 years (1889–1906) searching for Benito's treasure, but he only uncovered 33 gold coins! An explorer named Peter Bergman claimed to have discovered Benito's hoard in a remote cave in 1929. He was unable to remove much of the gold and silver, however, and when he tried to find the cave a second time he found it impossible to retrace his route. So, much of Benito's treasure still remains untouched. The last great treasure hunt on Isla del Coco took place in 1939. James Forbes, great-grandson of a crew member of the *Mary Dear*, began digging at a previously unexplored site. But he was unsuccessful and left the island with nothing to show for his efforts.

Did the most notorious pirates of the eighteenth century leave behind great stores of treasure that are yet to be discovered? Blackbeard Teach was a cruel and ruthless pirate who preyed on treasure ships in the Caribbean. In 1717, he buried a huge iron chest containing valuable booty

Blackbeard Teach watches two of his crewmen bury some of his treasure on the island of Plum. These men, along with four others from the crew, were later shot by Teach so that only he would know where the treasure lay.

Pirates attacking a merchant ship laden with a cargo of treasure.

on a small island called Plum. To make sure that no one could reveal its location, Teach shot the six helpers he had taken along. It was not until 1928 that two local fishermen on the island discovered a freshly dug hole with the imprint of a chest at the bottom. Had Teach's treasure been found?

In 1691, the wicked Captain William Kidd seized the precious cargo of the *Quedah Merchant*. Kidd buried gold bars and coins worth a huge sum of money on Gardiner's Island, New York. He was eventually caught, and during his trial he revealed where he had buried some of his treasure. Despite this cooperation, he was still sentenced to death. On the day before he was due to be hanged, Captain Kidd offered to reveal the whereabouts of the rest of the *Quedah Merchant's* treasure. His offer was refused because most people thought that little of the loot remained to be uncovered. But according to popular myth, Captain Kidd's treasure is still waiting to be found.

The sinking of the *Lusitania*

On May 7, 1915, during World War I, the British luxury passenger liner, the *Lusitania*, is steaming at over 20 knots off the south coast of Ireland. She carries over a thousand passengers together with a cargo of food and brass rods. She is also transporting over 4,000 cases of ammunition to Britain.

Captain William Turner is nervous because he knows that German submarines are active off the south coast of Ireland. At 2:11 p.m., the cry goes up, "Torpedo! Torpedo on the starboard side!" Within seconds it strikes the *Lusitania* below the bridge. Just 18 minutes later, the ship lies at the bottom of the ocean and 1,198 people are dead.

The sinking of the *Lusitania* marks a turning-point in World War I, for among those killed are 124 Americans. Their deaths help to bring the United States into the war against Germany. But mystery surrounds the incident even to this day. Were the *Lusitania* and her innocent passengers deliberately sacrificed in order to bring the United States into the war? Why was her escort of destroyers taken away, when it was known that German U-boats lay in her path? Did the liner sink so quickly because she was carrying an even larger, secret cargo of ammunition, which exploded when struck by the torpedo?

British Admiralty records covering the disaster were mysteriously "lost." But the suspicion remains that the *Lusitania* was lured into a trap designed by the British.

Conclusion

Ever since humans first looked out across the wide ocean and wondered what lay beyond the horizon, the sea has been a constant source of fascination and wonder for us. Ancient peoples imagined that the sea was a god, or the home of a number of gods, who controlled its various moods. Today, in the age of space travel and computers, few people believe such ideas. But the sea still remains beyond our control. It holds mysteries we cannot yet explain. It possesses secrets we may never unlock.

Mermaids, half-woman and half-fish, are said to live in the sea. Do they exist? They do — according to this nineteenth-century painting!

Left *We have always been fascinated by the hidden world beneath the oceans' waves. Here is a "diver" in the sixteenth century investigating underwater life.*

There may indeed be logical explanations to all the mysteries that have been discussed. The Bermuda Triangle contains some of the most heavily used shipping routes in the world. The losses in the area may be so high only because a lot of ships pass through it. It may be that the strange stories of ghosts and ghost ships are caused by mirages, hallucinations or overworked imaginations. The sea monsters that have caused so much terror may have been harmless manatees (animals a bit like whales). Those "monsters" that have claimed human victims may be no more than huge squid or whales.

Below *A mosaic (a picture made from colored pieces of stone) of Proteus, one of the ancient Greeks' gods of the sea.*

It is possible that stories of voyages to the Americas before Columbus are just legends. Perhaps archaeological discoveries may one day either prove or disprove these theories. Research and investigation may eventually clear up the mystery surrounding the sinking of the *Lusitania*, and the tales of buried pirate treasure.

An 8-meter (26-ft) squid was said to have been seen by Alecton's *crew off the Canary Islands on November 30, 1861. True or false?*

Stewart del.

But for the time being, you must make up your own mind. Is the sea the last great area of the unknown on earth, holding many secrets that await our discovery? Or are the mysteries of the sea no more than superstitions that have no place in the modern world? What do you think?

Above *Perhaps sea monsters are only angry whales?*

Below *One of the sea's secrets revealed: a part of the* Titanic's *deck.*

Glossary

Apex   The tip or highest point of a triangle.

Aristotle   A famous Greek philosopher and writer (384–322 BC).

Captain's log   Record of a ship's voyage kept by the captain.

Civilizations   Highly advanced peoples or races.

Epic   On a grand scale.

Hallucinations   Imagined experiences that appear to be real.

High technology   The most modern and efficient form of a particular piece of equipment.

Foundered   Filled with water and sank.

Galleon   A large Spanish trading ship.

Magnetic   Possessing an invisible force that attracts or repels certain objects.

Minerals   Substances in the earth that can be dug out and used (for example, coal, iron ore, gold and diamonds).

Mirage   Seeing something that does not exist.

Mutiny   A rebellion by a crew against its captain.

Mythical   Legendary.

Norse   Early Scandinavian.

Pastor   A local clergy man.

Plato   A famous Greek philosopher and writer (428–348 BC).

Salvager   Someone who recovers sunken or wrecked vessels.

Schooner   A rigged vessel with two or more masts.

Superstition   Fear of the unknown.

SOS   Literally "Save Our Souls"; the code sent out by a vessel in trouble.

Undulating   Moving up and down in gentle curves.

UFOs   Unidentified Flying Objects.

U-Boats   German submarines first used in World War I (from the German *Unterseebooten*, meaning undersea boats).

Visionary   Someone claiming to see the past or the future in his or her mind.

Captain William Kidd, the seventeenth-century pirate. Where did he bury the treasure he seized from the Quedah Merchant?

Further reading

Abranson, Eric, *Ships & Seafarers* Silver, Burdett, 1984

Berlitz, Charles, *The Bermuda Triangle* Avon, 1986

Braymer, Marjorie, *Atlantis: The Biography of a Legend* Atheneum, 1983

Dolan, Edward F., *The Bermuda Triangle and Other Mysteries of Nature* Franklin Watts, 1980

Heyerdahl, Thor, *Kon-Tiki* Rand McNally, 1984

Heyerdahl, Thor, *The Tigris Expedition: In Search of Our Beginnings* Doubleday, 1981

Jerome, Edward G., *Tales of Shipwreck* Pitman Learning, 1970

Larranaza, Robert D., *Pirates & Buccaneers* Lerner Publications, 1970

Marin, Albert, *The Sea Rovers: Pirates, Privateers & Buccaneers* Atheneum, 1984

McWilliams, Karen, *Pirates* Franklin Watts, 1989

The Kraken, a cross between a giant squid and an octopus. Does it really exist in our oceans' depths, or only in sailors' stories?

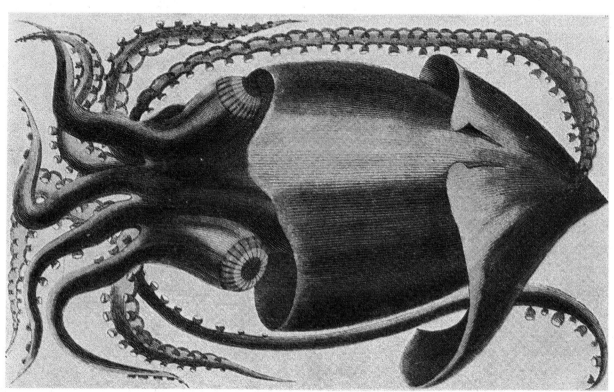

Index

Picture acknowledgments

The publishers would like to thank the following for supplying pictures for this book: Associated Press 45 (lower); Bruce Coleman Ltd 6 (upper: G. D. Plage; lower: Carl Roessler); Mary Evans Picture Library 28, 29, 32 (lower), 42, 46; Fortean Picture Library 17, 31 (lower), 32 (upper), 33 (Robert Le Serrec), 44; PHOTRI 22 (upper), 25; Ann Ronan Picture Library 45 (upper); Ronald Sheridan 22 (lower), 43 (both). The artwork is by the following people: Tony Gibbons *cover, frontispiece*, 8-9, 10, 13, 14-15, 18, 19, 24, 36, 37, 39, 40-41; Martin Kingstone 7, 11, 16, 20-21, 23, 26-7, 31, 34-5, 38; Stephen Wheele 32.